BODY AND SOUL

30 Day Devotional for Spiritual Health
and Fitness

By

Christopher Qualls

And

Justin Horton

I0143269

Christopher Qualls Publishing

Dedication

Christopher Qualls

For Dr. Deb Douglas:
Thank you. You impacted the world in incredible
ways, and it misses you painfully.

Most importantly, to Carrie, who is my partner for all
the nuance, texture and flavor of life. Words fail.
Thank you, my love.

Note from the Authors

As humans, we often struggle to comprehend the complexities of the spiritual realm. Walking with Christ can feel difficult, confusing and exhausting at times. Over many hours, and a lot of great coffee, authors Justin Horton and Christopher Qualls have discovered helpful ways to conceptualize spiritual growth, and help readers deepen their relationship with Christ.

We have discovered that, in our own lives, often times the discipline of our fitness pursuits has paralleled spiritual disciplines. Through physical pursuits like running, weight-lifting, yoga, meditation, sports, and the like, we have grown not only better and healthier, but also closer to God. It is our sincerest desire to share two of our greatest passions—spiritual and physical fitness—with others in the hopes that our journey might positively impact yours.

This devotional will give you new and unique perspectives with which to pursue spiritual maturation. Relating physical fitness to spiritual fitness, the authors facilitate spiritual discipline and development. Please enjoy this devotional, share it with friends, and remember to return to the material at any point in the future, particularly those times when one's spiritual journey seems static.

Introduction

For physical training is of some value, but Godliness holds value for all things, holding promise for both the present life and the life to come. 1 Timothy 4.8 (NIV)

We all want to be in shape. We all want to be healthy. We all want to be fit. But crash diets are dumb. Dieting often takes the approach of instant gratification. With a week-long crash diet, we believe we can lose those ten pounds before our beach vacation or fit into that tight dress. Statistically speaking, most dieters regain all or more of the weight they lose within two years. Without putting in meaningful work we won't see meaningful change. Christianity is like that. We often crave the changes that come along with being spiritually mature. We want to flaunt our spiritually sexiness, but we don't want to expend the effort (or time) to reach spiritual maturity. We seek the gifts of the spirit but not relationship with the spirit. We seek wisdom without consulting scripture. We seek intimacy without pursuing relationship. We seek meekness without becoming humble. In short, we seek the appearance of holiness and sanctification without truly encountering Jesus Christ (*Matthew 6.33*).

In physical fitness as with spiritual fitness we need life-change. Cutting sugar, fat, carbs, or calories is similar to trying to cut out sin; it's fine, but ineffectual and short-lived without sustainable holistic change. Much of the Church is busy struggling to sin less and missing out on what happens when we know God *more*. Countless times have I tried to pull sins out of my life, only to have them sneak right back into it. Anyone with a sweet-tooth who has tried to cut sweets from their diet knows the struggle. You're able to resist the temptation for a period, but eventually you hear those cookies calling your name and succumb. However, when we replace unhealthy with healthy habits, we begin to sustainably revolutionize our lives. Spiritual growth is not about cutting out sin like some sort of low carb diet; it is building a healthier lifestyle by developing one's personal relationship with Jesus Christ.

Before beginning, I encourage you to take some time and ask yourself a few questions:

- Where are you in your spiritual journey? Do you know?
- Where do you hope to go from where you are now? If you feel you have just begun, where should you start?

- How are you "working out"? How are you studying scripture? How are you trying to grow?
- Is Christian life new to you? Does it feel old or stagnant?

I hope that through this 30-day devotional you are able not only to further define your location on your spiritual journey, but I hope also to help you move closer to the ultimate destination: God's heart.

Through this devotional, we hope to facilitate an understanding of spiritual development that is beneficial to holistic spiritual growth and formation for Sons and Daughters of Jesus Christ. While we think it is important that you spend some time each day to reading and considering what we have written for you, nothing is a suitable substitute for spending time in the presence of the Lord. Prayer, meditation, worship, service--whatever facilitates intimacy between you and the spirit, do it!

Growth does not come from understanding the words in this text, but from relationship with the Father. At the bottom of each day's devotional we have provided several scriptures for further study. We suggest spending time reading and considering the implication of those scriptures in tandem with the provided thoughts of the day.

Remember, we do not live on bread alone, but on every word that comes from the father *(Deuteronomy 8.3; Matthew 4.4; Luke 4.4).*

Day 1
Purpose

Preach the word; be prepared in season and out of season; correct, rebuke and encourage--with great patience and careful instruction. 2 Timothy 4.2 (NIV)

What is the purpose of constantly challenging ourselves, physically or spiritually, to grow stronger? Why would we want to endure the strain? Why deprive ourselves of so many things for the sake of health? Why abstain from the pleasures of this world--like cake? The problem is not that a bite of cake will derail our fitness journey, nor is it that a missed devotion will cost us our relationship with Christ. The problem is preparedness.

What happens if you get thrust into a situation where you need to protect yourself or those you love, but you aren't prepared? How will you respond if your dog sprints out of the house and you are forced to run them down, but your legs and lungs are not up for the challenge? Contrary to popular belief (and Instagram), the purpose of fitness is not simply to look good enough to post proud selfies. Our goal is health. We want to be ready for whatever is thrown our way, in season and out of season.

All the training and sacrifice makes us much more capable to respond when we are called to action. Perhaps a co-worker is struggling with illness in their family. Maybe a friend confides in you their doubts. A family member could be ready to walk away from all of life's most beautiful and important things. Are you prepared?

We are told to preach the Word. Are you prepared?

We are told to correct, rebuke, and encourage. Are you prepared?

We are told to exhibit the fruit of the Spirit and heed careful instruction. Are you prepared?

Christ has a plan for your life. He never saves people to sit idly, but He adopts us into His family so that we may multiply, bringing more sons and daughters to join His Kingdom. It isn't about looking good. It is about internal health. Are you prepared?

For Further Study:

Preparedness
  Proverbs 6.6-8; Matthew 24.44; 1 Corinthians 16.13; 1 Peter 3.15

Day 2
First Day

There is neither Jew nor Gentile, neither slave nor free, nor is there male and female, for you are all one in Christ Jesus. Galatians 3.28 (NIV)

Do you remember walking into the gym for the first time? For most of us it was pretty intimidating. You may have needed a moment in the parking lot before entering to face the judgment of being out of shape. Finally, you go in. Not knowing the protocols, you fumble through the sign in process, walk into the bathroom and don't know where to put your stuff. Is every closed locker used? Is it ok if I open one to see if I can put my stuff there? Do I change here, or should I have changed before I got to the gym? Finally, you make it into the gym and all your worst fears are confirmed, but also you see others like you, who on January 1st decided to give it a shot. Of course, you came in without a plan: "Do I work out my chest, legs, or everything?" So, you make something up, jump on a machine, put on a generous amount of weight, and proceed to use that machine incorrectly, likely injuring yourself in the process. You see the looks of judgment from the regulars and leave, vowing to never return. Later, you wake up to the unexpected pain, further affirming your decision.

Conversely, maybe you are the regular gym-goer, dreading January 1st, when all the newbs take up your machines, despite having no idea how they operate. Maybe you switch your schedule to avoid this, until February 1st, when it's publicly acceptable to have failed one's resolution.

This is how unbelievers feel when they finally take the jump into a pew--completely clueless as to what to do and how to act. Protocols aren't listed, so they fumble through the service and never return, fearing judgment.

How are we greeting new believers? Are we welcoming them as brothers/sisters with joy, or are we stuck in routine and cliques? Let's welcome new believers, eager to show them the ropes and help them grow in the knowledge and love of our Lord and Savior!

For Further Study:

Welcoming
> Matthew 5.46-48; Romans 15.7; Matthew 25.35 - 36; Luke 9.11; Acts 15.4; 1 Samuel 25.6

Day 3
Soreness & Burn

He gives strength to the weary and increases the power of the weak. Isaiah 40.29 (NIV)

When we begin a new workout regimen, our body is incredibly sore. We feel it in every step. When changing our eating habits, we feel hunger pangs and cravings. There is pain involved in growth. Muscles grow because the fibers have been stretched, stressed, and broken down. Weight loss happens in the midst of those cravings. Gains come when we feel the burn. Strength comes through that soreness.

At those times when the Spirit calls us away from one habit, season, or influence and onto new things, there is initial resistance. Every attempt to stop sinning in a specific area is met with difficulty, and the enemy wants to see us fall away into disobedience. We must break the plane and move past the initial resistance to find freedom. There is soreness. There is a burn. This weariness is where we develop strength as a child of Christ.

We prove our mettle and our trustworthiness not by our impressive feats of strength, fortitude, or willpower. It is the daily toil where we work out our growth that we achieve worthiness.

These are the times that prepare us for outstanding moments of incredible faith. You will have struggle (*John 16.33*). Embrace the struggle and persevere, for it is then that you will grow complete, lacking nothing (*James 1.4*).

For Further Study:

Struggle
Psalm 34.19; Romans 5.3 & 12.12; Philippians 4.12-13; 1 Peter 1.6-9, 4.12, & 5.10; 2 Timothy 3.12 16; James 1.2-4 & v12

Strength
Joshua 1.9-10; 2 Chronicles 15.7-8; Philippians 4.7; 2 Corinthians 12.9

Day 4
Workout Partner

And let us consider how we may spur one another on toward love and good deeds, not giving up meeting together, as some are in the habit of doing, but encouraging one another--and all the more as you see The Day approaching. Hebrews 10.24-25 (NIV)

The first few times we go to the gym, it is difficult. It can feel like we walked into a place we don't belong. It can feel intimidating. When we start a diet, the first few days are daunting. When the cravings start to happen or the soreness kicks in, it can be all too easy to return to what is comfortable. Even when we have been working out for a while, we can get comfortable and stop pushing. A workout partner will recognize that and encourage us to do another rep, lift a few more pounds, or eat another healthy meal. They hold us accountable to make us better, faster, stronger.

Walking with Christ is hard. When we dedicate our lives to following the Spirit, things change. Change hurts. When we chafe against the winds of change, it is important to have a dedicated friend to spur us onward. More than a cheerleader--who shouts encouragement despite the state of the game--we need a partner, who will urge us to do more for the Kingdom and resist complacency.

We need people who will speak hard truths in the name of growth-giving feedback. Find someone in your life who loves you as you are, but too much to leave you that way. Find someone who will say the things you need to hear, like the prophet Nathan did to David (2 *Sam 12*).

We were designed by God to be in community *(Gen 2.18)*. We are our brothers' keepers *(Gen 4.9)*. We are supposed to be praying, eating, worshipping, and living life together *(Acts 2.42-47)*. This is how we have the chance to greatly impact one another's lives like iron sharpens iron *(Pro 27.17)*. Find a workout partner. Be a workout partner. Push yourself and others to grow stronger in the Spirit. Who do you know that can add value to your spiritual journey? What is preventing you from partnering with him or her?

For Further Study:

Community Responsibility
Psalm 133.1; Ecclesiastes 4.9-12; Matthew 18.20; John 13.20; Romans 12.4-5; Romans 15.5; 1 Corinthians 1.10; 1 Peter 3.8;1 John 4.11; Acts 4.32; Ezekiel 3.20; Proverbs 27.23; 1 John 4.21; Galatians 6.1-2; 1 Thessalonians 5.11

Day 5
Strength

Preach the word; be prepared in season and out of season; correct, rebuke and encourage--with great patience and careful instruction. 2 Timothy 4.2 (NIV)

For athletes, the purpose of strength training is clear: to prepare for competition. Football players lift to build strength for the game and runners seek distance to build stamina for race day. We all try to be conscientious of our eating to be better prepared for daily life, longevity, and whatever activities life throws our way. A successful competitor does not stop improving themselves. That is why many athletes spend hours each day lifting weights. Preparation is important.

As Christ followers, we must be mindful to build our spiritual health and strength for the trials and tribulations that will come. To do this, we must fail. Strength is built when muscles are damaged. There is pain involved. If we want to grow spiritually, we will take damage to our ego, among other things, and there will be times of discomfort. In fact, the most meaningful growth comes from the hard times--the two-a-days, if you will.

We must humble ourselves and be ready to receive rebukes, admonishments, and corrections. The Christian walk is just that--a walk. We should not be static. We should be growing continuously. That growth comes through testing our spiritual strength. Share the gospel. Be bold. Get out of your comfort zone. All the while, remain humble. Listen to brothers and sisters in Christ as teammates, remembering to receive critique and seek growth. Encourage others and be encouraged. Preparation takes time. No one can perfect their form without tolerating a little constructive feedback.

For Further Study:

Strength
Psalm 22.19, 28.7-8, 46.1 & 119.28; Isaiah 40.29 & 31; 2 Corinthians 12.9-10; Ephesians 3.16

Growth
Ephesians 4.15; Colossians 1.9-10; 1 Thessalonians 3:11-13; Hebrews 6.1-2; 2 Peter 1.5-7 & 3.17-18

Day 6
Exercise

No discipline seems pleasant at the time, but painful. Later on, however, it produces a harvest of righteousness and peace for those who have been trained by it. Therefore strengthen your feeble arms and weak knees. Hebrews 12.11-12 (NIV)

In the pursuit of fitness, there is no avoiding exercise. One must maintain some level of activity in order to burn calories, utilize muscles, and increase flexibility and range of motion. To engage in physical activity is an integral part of human health, even seemingly simple activities such as walking. Of course, too much exercise can have a negative effect. If more calories are burned than are taken in, it can result in serious health issues.

Spiritual growth also requires exercise. We must find an equilibrium between what we are consuming and what we actively do. With His last words, Christ mandated each of His followers to go and make disciples of all nations. How are you exercising your faith towards that end? What are you doing with your spiritual gifts? How are you serving your church, widows, orphans, people experiencing poverty, homelessness, addiction, hunger, or disease?

If we exercise too much, we will reach a point of diminishing returns. Instead of seeing gains, or growth, our body begins to digest itself. Of course, many of us are all too familiar with the perils of too little exercise; no growth happens if we aren't putting in the work.

We are healthiest and growing when our exercise is related to our intake, or, as it is often conceptualized, when we pour out from our overflow. How are you exercising? Do you need to evaluate the health of your exercise or your intake? Should you find a healthier balance between the two?

For Further Study:

Faith in Action
Psalm 90.17; James 1.22-25 & 2.14-18; John 13.17; Colossians 3.23-24; Matthew 7.21 & 25:31-46

Day 7
Practice

[B]eing confident of this, that He who began a good work in you will carry it on to completion until the day of Christ Jesus. Philippians 1.6 (NIV)

All good things take time. No one has the footwork of Lionel Messi the first time they touch a soccer ball. Kids don't hit the pool swimming like Michael Phelps. Ask any Olympian and they will tell you that years of dedication, training, and sacrifice are responsible for their success. Skills are honed by experience and learning. Bodies are shaped over long arcs of time. We are today the accumulation of all that has happened before this day. It is unfair to ourselves to demand that we change it all tomorrow.

Spiritual growth occurs over time. There will be moments when it feels like something simply clicks into place. It's as if blinders fell from our spiritual eyes and suddenly things are so clear. Those moments, too, are the product of working out our faith over time.

Seemingly more regular is the feeling that we are going nowhere fast. The frustration of feeling stagnant when we yearn and strive for growth can often be the very thing that limits that growth. When you feel frustrated by the struggle, do not give up on the routine, training, discipline, dedication, and sacrifice, but have faith that He who began a good work in you will carry it on to completion--*until the day of Christ Jesus.*

If Jesus has not returned yet and you are alive, you are still a work in progress and therefore have no business giving up on daily disciplines towards spiritual growth.

For Further Study:

Diligence/Time
> 1 Timothy 4.15;1 Peter 1.13; 2 Peter 1.10-11 & 3.14; Galatians 6.9; Hebrews 12.1; Revelations 1.13

Growth
> Job 17.9; Psalm 84.7 & 92.12; Proverbs 4.18; Acts 9.22; Ephesians 4.14-15; 1 Corinthians 13.11; Hebrews 5.14 & 6.1; 1 Peter 2.2; 2 Peter 3.18

Day 8
Sick Gains

Remain in me, as I also remain in you. No branch can bear fruit by itself; it must remain in the vine. Neither can you bear fruit unless you remain in me.
John 15.4 (NIV)

It is such a justifying feeling when someone recognizes from your body that you have adapted your habits to promote a healthier lifestyle. Someone comments about how you've lost weight or how you've gained muscle, and it feels so gratifying. The growth, which you can feel within your body, has made its way to the outside, and people are beginning to notice! That is payoff.

Jesus tells us that we will know His followers by their fruits. Fruit is produced in our lives in accordance with where we are rooted. We might produce good fruit or bad fruit, but if we are rooted in Christ, we should be producing the good fruit of the Spirit: love, joy, peace, patience, kindness, goodness, faithfulness, gentleness, and self-control. We should be fruitful, multiplying our number of believers. We should propagate life, as does fruit.

At the time when our lives begin to reflect the person of Christ, others will notice. What we have felt from within ourselves will become manifest outwardly. This is spiritual growth-- that one's good fruit should be so visible to the world that the Father receives praise for the transformative work He has done, reviving a dead branch.

For Further Study:

Fruit
Matthew 3.8, 7.15-20, 12.33 & 13.23; Luke 3.8-9 & 8.15; John 15; Romans 7.4-5; Philippians 1.9-11; Titus 3.4; James 2.14-26 & 3.7; Hebrews 12.10-11

Spiritual Fruit
Galatians 5.13-25

Day 9
Leg Day

Therefore, my dear friends, as you have always obeyed--not only in my presence, but now much more in my absence--continue to work out your salvation with fear and trembling. Philippians 2.12 (NIV)

We have all seen those people at the gym who've focused so much on bulking up the top half of their body, but they neglect their legs. Leg day can be tough, and the few days after working out your legs can be even harder. But nobody wants to have ripped arms and chest paired with tiny chicken legs like they might topple over. It isn't hard to imagine that those who neglect to grow their legs always wear pants, as if to cover up and hide their inadequacies. That is why friends don't let friends skip leg day.

Are you working in what is comfortable, or are you pushing beyond yourself? If we always operate within what is easy, how will we grow? It is natural to have strengths and weaknesses. Perhaps you have a gift or talent that is comfortable, but you also have legs. If you cover them up, who will know about those gifts? It is necessary to have a strong foundation upon which to build, but inherent in this idea is the implication that we build beyond the foundation--we grow. The parts of your faith which you actively work out are the foundation but consider new exercises--new routines--which foster growth in new areas.

Cultivate each spiritual fruit. Learn spiritual disciplines. Study all spiritual gifts. God has chosen and included you in His plan for the reconciliation of humanity; you are the tool the artist uses to shape His masterpiece. How inefficient to have an obstinate tool adamant about only one thing to the detriment of the entire art piece.

For Further Study:

Growth
> Job 17.9; Psalm 84.7 & 92.12; Proverbs 4.18; Acts 9.22; Ephesians 4.14-15; 1 Corinthians 13.11; Hebrews 5.14 & 6.1; 1 Peter 2.2; 2 Peter 3.18

Spiritual Fruit
> Galatians 5.13-25

Day 10
Good and Bad Pain

In the same way, the Spirit helps us in our weakness. We do not know what we ought to pray for, but the Spirit Himself intercedes for us with groans that words cannot express. Romans 8.26 (NIV)

In exercise there is a good pain and a bad pain. Many people appreciate the soreness that comes after a long run or a good workout. That type of pain seems to congratulate a strong performance. It is the harbinger of growth--of pushing beyond what was previously limiting. There is another pain that brings less appreciated news. The pain of correction alerts the body to a problem. Rather than congratulate tenacity and diligence, it acts as a caution sign telling us to stop before things become problematic. Injury pain says you are messing up and should stop, or that you have previously made a mistake.

When we break the plane of negative habits in our lives--when we grow in Christ--we can often chafe against the winds of change. Upsetting the spiritual inertia that has held us in place for so long feels uncomfortable, but it ultimately leads to spiritual growth. On the other hand, conviction is the pain in our spirit when we need correction. The Holy Spirit reacts to a sin

behavior and alerts us to the need for change.
To heed the Spirit in this moment means avoiding more serious injury, but to disobey puts our spirit in need of healing.

Conviction comes from the Spirit to shape us into the men and women God designed us to be. When that uncomfortable feeling enters into our spirit, it is a sure sign that something is being done improperly and requires a change. It is imperative that we listen when the Holy Spirit brings us this corrective pain, lest we end up quenching the Spirit, thereby seriously injuring ourselves and our spiritual walk. Just as in the gym, we must learn to discern between feeling the burn of a strong performance, and the pain that precedes injury.

For Further Study:

Correction
> Job 5.17; Proverbs 3.12; Psalm 49.12; Ephesians 5.11-13; 2 Timothy 3.16; Hebrews 12.6

Conviction
> John 16.8; Romans 8.5-6; 1 John 2.20; 1 Thessalonians 5.19

Spiritual Growth
> Romans 12.2; Jude 1.20; Ephesians 4

Holy Spirit
> Titus 3.6; Romans 8.26

Day 11
Results

I will give you a new heart and put a new spirit in you; I will remove from you your heart of stone and give you a heart of flesh. Ezekiel 36.26 (NIV)

Have you ever tried a highly restrictive diet? The list of things not to be eaten can be so long that the easiest explanation might be to imagine everything you want and assume you can't have it. These diets require a healthy amount of sacrifice and even more discipline. It can be easy to imagine staggering results like weight loss, lower body fat percentage, or smaller pant size. Often, the physical results are middling, but we are left feeling incredible!

The result of countless meals with restrictions and hours of shopping, food prep, and cooking is not only seen on the outside of the body, but also on the inside. The body begins functioning better than ever, with energy abounding. Mentally, emotionally, and physically, we feel at peak health. The true transformation occurs within. It takes time, effort, and discipline--as do most things of value. Surely you have experienced this in your workouts, diets, training, etc.

When Christ makes us into a new creation--

when we set out on our spiritual journey--there will be transformation. Certain things will happen at once, but for others, conversion can take time. As you continue to grow your relationship with the Father, He will regularly be renewing you. Results may not be easily visible in your life but know that the Spirit is creating in you a new heart. Be encouraged: though there are times spiritual growth seems imperceptible, remain diligent and be aware that Christ is doing a work within you that He will see through to completion (*Philippians 1.6*).

For Further Study:

Renewal
Psalm 51.10; Romans 12.1-2; 2 Corinthians 4.16 & 5.17; Ephesians 4.22-24; Colossians 1.21-23

Day 12
Seen and Unseen

Woe to you, teachers of the law and Pharisees, you hypocrites! You are like whitewashed tombs, which look beautiful on the outside but on the inside are full of bones of the dead and everything unclean. In the same way, on the outside you appear to people as righteous but on the inside you are full of hypocrisy and wickedness. Matthew 23.27-28 (NIV)

It can be tempting to think that someone is healthy because they have an envious body type. Likewise, we might assume that because someone doesn't look like a fitness model, it follows that they are unhealthy. However, we all know people who subsist on junk food, but never seem to gain weight. There are also people who call themselves vegetarians because they don't eat meat. Of course, Twinkies and french fries aren't meat, but they aren't nutritious, either.

As followers of Christ, we sometimes focus too much on the exterior. We think that what matters is that which is seen. Health, however, can be unseen. It is the interior that matters.

Muscles get stronger before they get bigger. Habitual dietary improvements come before meaningful body changes. Interior health promotes exterior changes. Do not be fooled into fixing the exterior and neglecting the interior. That is not how true health is achieved.

Jesus calls the religious elite whitewashed tombs because they fell into the trap of believing that health was only what was seen. They neglected the unseen work of the inner person—the work of the soul. In order to experience true transformation and genuine health, we must be focused on the internal. Transformation flows from within. Allow the Spirit of God to have complete control in the interior worlds of your heart, mind, and soul, and behaviors follow.

For Further Study:

Inner person
2 Corinthians 4.16; 1 Samuel 16.7; Proverbs 20.27; Ephesians 3.16-20; Colossians 3.5-10; Psalm 51.6

Day 13
Training

Everyone who competes in the games goes into strict training. They do it to get a crown that will not last; but we do it to get a crown that will last forever. 1 Corinthians 9.25 (NIV)

Several times throughout Scripture our calling is related to a race. Can you imagine competing in a marathon, never having trained? Your body would not be prepared. Respiratory, circulatory, skeletal, and muscular systems would not be properly equipped to handle the strain. Athletes use their offseason not for downtime, but to prepare for game day. Even professionals spend the offseason going to training camps to build strength, agility, dexterity, balance, lung capacity, etc. The fact is simple: if you want to succeed, you train.

Prepare to run the race that is marked out for you by practicing your faith. Don't allow your beliefs to sit dormant within you; activate your faith! Belief without action is hardly a strong belief (*James 2.14-26*). Like a professional, be ready to compete--working diligently even outside the season of your calling--training to be better, faster, and stronger. In this Christian journey, your competition comes not from Christian brothers and sisters, but from the enemy, who prowls like a lion (*1 Peter 5.8*).

Be disciplined in training, always growing stronger in the Spirit. Your opponent takes no days off. Though there will be seasons where your abilities are not called upon--seasons where you sit the bench--there will also be seasons when you are called upon to enter the game. When your time comes, will you be prepared?

For Further Study:

Race
> Acts 20.24; 2 Timothy 4.1-8; Hebrews 12.1-3

Seasons
> Ecclesiastes 3.1-8; 2 Timothy 4.2

Preparedness
> Matthew 25.1-13; Luke 8.13; Romans 12.12;
> Ephesians 4.11-17; James 1.2-8; 2 Timothy 4.2

Day 14
Body Types

There are many parts, but one body. 1 Corinthians 12.20 (NIV)

Chapters 12 through 14 of 1 Corinthians discuss the various spiritual attributes distributed to those who have the Holy Spirit, referring regularly to the collection of believers--the church--as the body of Christ, who is the head. Rightly so, that body cannot be made of all the same part. Have you ever seen someone made entirely out of thumbs? Without diversity in the body, we would be nonfunctional. This necessarily means that there are differences between the parts of the body. I may be gifted spiritually to be a mouth while you may be gifted to be hands. Either way, there is still a call for unity, reminding each part that it needs all the others.

Comparison is tempting. Physically, we may look around and feel there is always someone stronger, fitter, thinner, or more flexible. Plenty of highly capable people have left teams, gyms-- and, yes, churches--because they felt intimidated, incapable, or outmatched. In the body of Christ, we must realize that there is diversity.

In football, an offensive lineman will look very different than a running back, and that is an important difference. The offensive line requires a different body type so that they can stop the defense. We are equipped and gifted uniquely, but intentionally. These giftings work together to accomplish God's plan. There should be no exclusion for that, but instead, unity. Find how we can work together, as one body lead by the head--Jesus--to do His will.

Avoid falling into the trap of comparison. Your spiritual body type--your equipping and gifting--is exactly what the Father has chosen for you to have so that you may, at appointed times, serve the purposes which He intended for you. Celebrate, be proud, and utilize those talents to edify and grow the church.

For Further Study:

Spiritual Giftings
Romans 12.3-8; 1 Corinthians 12-14; Ephesians 4.1-16; 1 Peter 4.7-11

Comparison/Jealousy
Proverbs 14.30; 1 Corinthians 3.3 & 10.3; Philippians 2.3; James 3.14-16 & 4.11

Day 15
Personal Trainer

Be imitators of me as I am of Christ. 1 Corinthians 11.1 (NIV)

Anyone who has ever had a personal trainer is intimately familiar with the idea of discipleship. Trainers have already had the experience of getting healthy and fit. They have demystified the secrets, perfected the moves, and fully adopted the thought patterns necessary to be at peak performance. Through whatever means are successful, they then attempt to pass this information on to others who are earlier on their health and fitness journey, so as to help them hone the practices more quickly.

As Paul writes to the church in Corinth, he encourages them to imitate him as he follows Christ. Our end goal isn't to act like Paul, however. It is to imitate Christ. Likewise, when we find a personal trainer, our goal is not to be like him or her. We are following their example to become healthier.

As we journey ever closer to the heart of the Father, it can be immensely beneficial to have a personal trainer a mentor or discipler. There are many struggles, mistakes, and experiences through which another Christian might have come.

That knowledge and wisdom can save you untold heartache. The enemy is not so creative. He has used the same traps since the garden, though he dresses them up differently. Through the admonishment, encouragement, feedback, and teaching of a spiritual personal trainer, we might grow stronger more quickly, with fewer setbacks.

If you do not have someone like this in your life, prayerfully begin seeking out someone older in the faith who might harness those experiences they have had to help you on your journey. It is dangerous to go alone.

For Further Study:

Mentorship
> Psalm 145.4; Proverbs 1.5, 9.9, 13.20, & 27.17;
> Philippians 2.1-8; Titus 2.3-5; Hebrews 13.7;
> 1 Peter 5.5-7 & 5.15

Discipleship
> Luke 6.40 & 9.23; John 8.31-32; Acts 8.30-31;
> 2 Timothy 2.2

Examples:
> The boy Samuel; Joshua and Moses; Paul and
> Timothy

Day 16
Fatigue

But few things are needed--or indeed only one. Mary has chosen what is better, and it will not be taken away from her. Luke 10.42 (NIV)

Imagine going to the gym day in and day out for weeks. You're not resting. You're burning calories at a faster rate than you're taking them in. Imagine, too, that you've cut calories to a fraction of your daily intake. If this is your plan, you're headed for disaster.

Far too frequently do well-intentioned Christians overwork themselves into fatigue. Martha spent her time cleaning and preparing for Jesus, while Mary spent time in Jesus' presence. We are called to action, but never to the detriment of relationship.

In His last days, Jesus likens Himself to bread. He tells us to pray for our daily bread. If we are overworking ourselves, we are using up the sustenance that comes from spending time in His presence.

Are you trying to pour out more than you contain? Are you trying to burn spiritual calories you don't have? The solution to burnout and spiritual fatigue is to rest in the presence of the

Lord. Recline with Christ daily. By intentional relationship, consume the bread that gives you life. His body, broken for you, will sustain you. Learn from Martha and Mary and take a break from frantic doing to rest in the presence of the perfect Father. Rest your head on His chest; sit at His feet. Get intimate with Him, for it is that relationship that sustains the soul in trying times.

For Further Study:

Overworking
Genesis 2.1-4; Exodus 18.13-24 & 23.12; Psalm 127.2; Luke 10.38-42; Ecclesiastes 2.22-23 & 5.16-17

Rest
Psalm 55.6 & 62.1; Matthew 11.28-30; Mark 6.31; Hebrews 4.9-11

Lord's Prayer
Matthew 6.9-13; Luke 11.2-4

Bread (Relationship)
Deuteronomy 8.3; Isaiah 30.20; Matthew 4.4 & 26.26; Luke 22.19; John 6.31, v35, v48 & v51

Day 17
Rest

There remains, then, a Sabbath-rest for the people of God; for anyone who enters God's rest also rests from his own work, just as God did from His. Let us, therefore, make every effort to enter that rest, so that no one will fall by following their example of disobedience. Hebrews 4.9-11 (NIV)

We need rest, physically and spiritually. Jesus often sought out quiet and calm. God demonstrated for us the practice of rest and asked us to follow suit. Rest is important. Our bodies can go a week without food. We cannot go a week without sleep. Rest will allow our muscular system to rest and heal after a good workout, locking in the gains. Not only does sleep heal the muscles, but it also restores the brain. Some studies suggest that sleep makes us more mentally alert, capable of remembering, creative, and intelligent. If the Creator took care to design humans in such a way that rest has wonderful benefits for the body, *and* He modeled the practice asked of us, we might need to pay attention.

Rest can be a tricky thing to define. For some, rest looks like simply being sedentary. For others, that won't do. Spiritual rest can take many forms, and it can be challenging to discern just which is the best for you. The idea, though, is to be refreshed and rejuvenated spiritually. It can look like varying up your spiritual regime. If you always serve at church, take some time off to get into God's presence by meditating, intimate worship, or prayer. If you regularly preach or teach, offer your platform to someone seeking that experience and open yourself to what the Spirit will say through that person to you. Light candles, blare worship music, and sit on the floor, quietly and still. Spiritual rest can look different, but it always involves becoming intimate with the Spirit.

For Further Study:

Rest

Genesis 2.3; Exodus 20.8-10 & 33.14; Ecclesiastes 4.6; Psalm 3.5, 37.7, 46.10,55.6, 62.1, & 91.1; Isaiah 26.3, 30.15 & 40.29-31; Jeremiah 31.25; Matthew 11.28-30; Mark 1.35 & 6.31; Acts 3.20-21; Hebrews 4.9-10

Day 18
Protein

But solid food is for the mature, who by constant use have trained themselves to distinguish between good and evil. Hebrews 5.14 (NIV)

Throughout the ministry of Jesus, and, in fact, throughout the Scriptures, we see the Word of God referred to as spiritual food. Here it says that solid food is for the mature. By contrast, milk is for those who are not yet ready for spiritual food *(1 Corinthians 3.2; Hebrews 5.12-13).* Infants of many species are given milk. It is wonderful for initial growth and development, and it is provided to most infants without requiring much work in return. However, at a certain point, that infant must begin to secure his or her own nutrition, beyond that provided by milk. Carnivores and herbivores must learn to hunt for nutritious sustenance that promotes growth and maturity.

If we desire to grow in Christ, we must stop subsisting on Sunday sermons alone. Pastors are shepherds. They watch over a heard and strive to protect it, but it is not the job of the shepherd to ensure the sheep eat grass. The responsibility falls upon us to learn to hunt. If we desire spiritual growth, we must find spiritual meat-- protein to build spiritual muscles. This can be found in a myriad of ways, but perhaps none is more nutritious than personally consuming the words of God. To grow we must learn to feed ourselves outside that which is provided by pastors. Find spiritual nutrients in the Scriptures and intimate time with the Father. Learn to hunt for yourself, in whatever way works best for you, but you must stop passively allowing yourself to be spoon-fed.

For Further Study:

Spiritual Milk
   1 Corinthians 3.2; Hebrews 5.12-14; 1 Peter 2.2

Scripture as Food
      Deuteronomy 8.3; Matthew 4.4; Luke 4.4; 1 Corinthians 10.1-4

Day 19
Obesity

In the same way, faith, by itself, if it is not accompanied by action, is dead. James 2.17 (NIV)

Pharisees and Sadducees were puffed up with knowledge, but often lacking in the realm of meaningful activity. They consumed tons of information about the Scriptures, but the New Testament paints them as rarely acting obediently. Our own spirits can easily become obese, much like those of the Pharisees, when we sit at church to be spiritually fed but engage in no spiritual activity.

The body needs about 2,000 calories to sustain average daily activity. We consume those calories when we eat food, which gives us energy. If we have a drastic calorie surplus, meaning we are taking in much more than we are burning through our regular activity, the result is weight gain. Too frequently do we find ourselves consuming large spiritual meals, full of spiritual calories, but failing to actively burn that spiritual energy. We need to practice those things we are learning from our pastors, devotionals, small groups, etc. Without activating our faith, we run the risk of being spiritually puffed up, like the Pharisees of Jesus' day.

How then do we justify gorging our spirits on weekly sermons, daily devotionals, revivals, retreats, or the like, while simultaneously resting our spirits? Our faith needs exercise! Use the gifts the Spirit has given you to build the Kingdom and edify the church. Preach the good news. Extend love to others. Serve. Witness. There are countless ways to exercise your faith. God has created us each uniquely and we have a unique part to play in His plan for the Kingdom. Without exercising those gifts, your part is missing. The Father and His bride desire for you to join the team, without fear or hesitation, lest you become spiritually obese like the Pharisees and Sadducees of Jesus' time.

For Further Study:

Strength

Psalm 22.19, 28.7-8, 46.1 & 119.28; Isaiah 40.29 & 31; 2 Corinthians 12.9-10; Ephesians 3.16

Growth

Ephesians 4.15; Colossians 1.9-10; 1 Thessalonians 3:11-13; Hebrews 6.1-2; 2 Peter 1.5-7 & 3.17-18

Day 20
Gluttony

Give us this day our daily bread. Matthew 6.11
(NIV)

If Jesus took the time to give us a format for how to pray, we ought to pay attention to it. In the format of the prayer He modeled, He specifically asks for today's daily bread. This suggests that there is enough bread to satisfy daily, but we cannot buy or eat a loaf today and be sustained by it tomorrow. Implicit in this prayer is the idea that children of Christ are to return to Him daily for their spiritual sustenance. The Israelites experienced a similar situation when their trust in God was tested daily by His provision of manna from heaven. If the manna was stored up, it would go bad overnight.

We cannot binge on Sunday services, conferences, retreats, or summer camps. Regularly--daily, in fact--we should return to the source of our rest and our strength to be renewed by our relationship with the Creator God. If we attempt to sustain our spirit on last week's meal, we will easily become depleted and sickened, just as if we attempted to jog five miles without having eaten recently. Neither would you attempt to lift having fasted for several days.

Our body is fueled by energy from regular meals to sustain activity.

Your spirit is fueled by energy from regular time with God, whether through prayer and meditation, studying Scripture, intimate worship or whatever gets you close with the Father.

For Further Study:

Rest
　Psalm 55.6 & 62.1; Matthew 11.28-30; Mark 6.31;
Hebrews 4.9-11

Lord's Prayer
Matthew 6.9-13; Luke 11.2-4

Bread (Relationship)
Deuteronomy 8.3; Isaiah 30.20;
Matthew 4.4 & 26.26; Luke 22.19;
John 6.31, 35, 48 & 51

Day 21
Junk Food

Finally, brothers, whatever is true, whatever is noble, whatever is right, whatever is pure, whatever is lovely, whatever is admirable--if anything is excellent or praiseworthy--think about such things. Philippians 4.8 (NIV)

Food is fuel for our bodies. Long distance runners might load up on carbohydrates before a race, then fuel--eat snacks--during the race. Weightlifters understand their body's need for protein to build muscle. Many diets are built around the concept of consuming cleaner, rather than less, fuel. It is an established fact that the type of fuel you input will affect the performance output. If you don't believe that, try eating fast food before you exercise.

Our spirits have a similar input to output system. When we begin to lose focus on the Father, we will start to feel a subtle distance drifting into the relationship. Remain in the practice of staying spiritually disciplined. Consume the word of God. Pursue authentic relationships with godly people. Meditate on things of the Spirit. Wait in God's presence. These are the things your spirit craves. When this is your fuel, your performance output will yield strong spiritual results.

Problems arise when our input is devoid of spiritual nutrition, or worse. If all one consumes is popular TV shows, movies, and music, never returning to seek spiritually healthy things, where will nutrition come from? How can we grow stronger or healthier?

For Further Study:

Scripture as Food
> Deuteronomy 8.3; Matthew 4.4; Luke 4.4;
> John 6.51; 1 Corinthians 10.1-4

Day 22
Appetite

He humbled you, causing you to hunger and then feeding you with manna, which neither you nor your ancestors had known, to teach you that man does not live on bread alone but on every word that comes from the mouth of the Lord. Deuteronomy 8.3 (NIV)

Hunger lets us know that we need more energy. As the caloric energy has been burned off throughout our activities, there comes a time when we realize we need sustenance. The presence of God--interaction with His living Word or His Holy Spirit--these satisfy our spiritual appetite. How then will we feel spiritual hunger if we are not active? Scripture is clear that healthy spirituality needs not only faith, but also works, nor is works alone enough (*James 2.14-26*).

In several seasons throughout life, we will find ourselves with seemingly no appetite. Craving the things of God feels distant. Consider your metabolism, activity level and intake, and apply discipline, just as one would for physical fitness. Be diligent not to skip regular consumption of spiritual energy. Be wary that you do not stop acting out your faith in service to others, love, and justice. A balance must be found. In the times our spirits do not compellingly yearn for spiritual growth, we must put into place a structure conducive to goals of growth.

Weightlifters striving for gains in muscle mass will often consume incredible amounts of protein. Olympians eat enormous meals, full of calories, before a competition. Runners load their body with carbohydrates. Undoubtedly there are times when the idea of another sip of a protein shake, bite of eggs, or fork full of pasta seems detestable, but there is a race marked out for us and it involves growth (*Hebrews 12.1-3*). If we are to successfully run, we must also diligently consume and train.

For Further Study:

Hunger
Psalm 81.10; Nehemiah 9.15; Matthew 4.4 & 5.6;
Luke 4.4; John 6.33-35; 1 Peter 2.2

Bread
Isaiah 30.20; Matthew 4.4 & 26.26; Luke 22.19;
John 6.31, 35, 48 & 51

Day 23
Plateau Effect

Therefore let us move beyond the elementary teachings about Christ and be taken forward to maturity, not laying again the foundation of repentance from acts that lead to death, and of faith in God. Hebrews 6.1 (NIV)

If you have ever set fitness goals, you are acquainted with the idea of the plateau effect, which is similar to that of diminishing returns. What once worked to shape muscles, improve speed, or lose weight may begin to yield little to no result. This has given rise to popular interval training and muscle confusion techniques for physical fitness. If we are to be known by our fruit (*Matthew 7.16*), but we are not producing, then something needs to change (*Luke 13.7-9*).

Overcome the plateau effect with a few techniques, not the least of which is discipline.

Romans 10.17 says faith comes from hearing the word of Christ. If you find that you are not regularly working your spiritual muscles by lifting your Bible, this is a great place to start. If you feel stagnant but have regularly been studying Scripture--switch it up. Take a page from the muscle confusion playbook and study Scripture differently. God has something to say to you.

Mark 6.7 tells us that Jesus Himself sent the disciples out two-by-two. If Christ thought that the disciples needed community, we probably do too. Find a spiritual workout partner to encourage you onward and hold you accountable. Remember friends, don't let friends skip leg day. If you're struggling to grow spiritually, there is little better for it than authentic community rich with feedback.

Matthew 28.19-20 commands that the followers of Christ go, make disciples, baptize, and teach. We were not saved to sit; we were saved to serve. If you are not actively discipling someone, sharing the Gospel, and teaching people about your faith, you will undoubtedly see stagnation. With His last words on earth, Jesus tells His followers that this is what He has left for them to do. If we aren't doing it, we cannot expect to grow.

Day 24
Detox

But Jesus often withdrew to lonely places and prayed.
Luke 5.16 (NIV)

Physically and spiritually, there are benefits to detoxification. For periods of time, I try to cut from my diet added sugars, processed or fried foods, or red meat. Many people start their year out with an annual cleanse. Social media and technology are other things from which I must periodically remove myself. The point of a detox is not to get a reward like weight loss, however. The purpose is to become more of who God designed us to be.

When we detoxify our lives and spirits for the Lord, it should not be an exchange. "God, I will give up food, social media, or a behavior if you answer all my questions." Our aim should be to give up the things that distract us from our relationship with the Father in exchange for time to focus on Him. Throughout His ministry, Jesus withdrew to find solitude and encouraged the disciples to follow suit. Much like the body needs time to rest and recover before it is pushed to its limits, Jesus often withdraws just before or just after doing miracles, healings, preaching to large crowds, etc. Not because Jesus needed answers from God--He is one with God--but because He desired intimacy with God.

Diets tend to be ineffective over the long term. Real change happens when we adjust our habits in such a way that we become the person God has designed us to be. Detoxing our spirit is not a short-term solution to hardship, but rather a practice that can foster intimacy with the Father, who can shape us into the person He means for us to be. Set time aside daily to spend in solitude with the Father, free of toxic distractions. Consider making it a regular practice in your life to sacrifice your often spiritually toxic social media platforms in exchange for more intimate solitude.

For Further Study:

Solitude
> Psalm 39.2-5, 46.10; Isaiah 30.15; Jeremiah 9.2; Matthew 6.6; Galatians 5.25

Jesus' Example
> Matthew 4.1-11, 14.13 & 23, & 17.1-9; Mark 1.35 & 6.30-32 & 45-46; Luke 4.42, 6.12, & 9.28

Day 25
Daily Meals

Jesus answered, "It is written: 'Man shall not live on bread alone, but on every word that comes from the mouth of God.'" Matthew 4.4 (NIV)

When the Israelites were wandering through the desert for 40 years, food was scarce. As an act of provision, God caused a sort of bread to be provided for them each day. Miraculous though it was, the bread would not stay fresh beyond one day. His people were forced to rely upon Him every single day for their life-sustaining provision. Understanding this history puts into context when Jesus tells us to pray for "daily bread."

The Father wants to provide for you. He has wisdom, insights, and intimacy that He wants to share with you. Like the Israelites, you must learn to daily rely upon Him to provide sustenance for your soul. Where we get into trouble is when our spirits have not tasted His provision in weeks. Scripture has been provided for us and has the power to replenish our spirit. Spending time in the presence of God in worship, meditation, and/or adoration can replenish our spirit. Being in community with believers can replenish our spirit. One thing, however, that does not replenish us is day-old bread.

Do not rely on revelation or intimacy from last week, month, or year. Rather, discipline yourself to consume nutritional spiritual meals regularly, just as you have several daily meals. It is not the lifting of weights which builds up muscles. In fact, working out tears down muscle fibers. What we consume is what builds up and shapes us. Neither the body nor the spirit was intended to gorge Sunday and starve for six days. Be diligent about spiritual nutrition.

For Further Study:

Bread

Isaiah 30.20; Matthew 26.26; Luke 22.19; John 6.31, v35, v48 & v51

Lord's Prayer

Matthew 6.9-13; Luke 11.2-4

Provision of Manna

Exodus 16

Day 26
Lifestyle Change

Set your minds on things above, not on earthly things. Colossians 3.2 (NIV)

Have you ever tried eating healthy? The beginning is hard! Every time you're eating a salad or something without cheese (can I get an amen?) all you think about is queso or fried food. Usually, this temptation stops diets within the first week or so, but if you push past that barrier, you can feel your body craving healthy food--something that two weeks ago would have seemed absurd! I've been there. People thought I was crazy for craving salads, but I did. Eventually, for many of us, there comes a day we cave. Thirty minutes to an hour later our bodies remind us what a bad choice we made, even though a month ago, the same food wouldn't have affected us.

Colossians reminds us that we can set our affections on godly things and change our desires. I'm not suggesting it will be easy, but with Christ, it is possible. As you continue to read, you will see all of what Christ calls us to abandon, and how sweet is the freedom from those desires and temptations.

The world would love us to believe that we are

who we are--that change is too much to ask--but that is not what we see in the Word. Romans 12.2 shows that we are called to "*...be transformed by the renewal of your mind...*" Paul points out this takes time and effort: "*...that by testing you may discern what is the will of God.*"

Let us turn from the things the hinder, push through the waves of temptation and begin to crave the things of Christ.

For Further Study:

Transformation
2 Corinthians 5.17-21; Romans 5.1-21; Psalm 51.10-12; Psalm 139.23-24; Ezekiel 36.26; Romans 12.2

Turn from/to
Galatians 5.19-26

Temptation
Ephesians 6.10-13

Day 27
Hydrate

Jesus answered, "Everyone who drinks this water will be thirsty again, but whoever drinks the water I give them will never thirst. Indeed, the water I give them will become in them a spring of water, welling up to eternal life." John 4.13-14 (NIV)

Hydration is more important even than food. Your body can go up to three weeks without food but can only survive about three to four days without water. At least 60% of the body is water, and every single cell in the body needs it to function. Fluids allow our joints to move with ease, regulate temperature, and flush negative or unneeded things as waste. Going a few days without food can be uncomfortable; going a few days without water can be fatal.

Peak health and fitness require diligent consumption of fluids. You'll often see athletes carrying around huge jugs or bottles of water with times scrawled on the side to help them pace their intake. Dehydration during muscle strain can lead to cramps, headaches, confusion, anger, fever, and blurred vision. Imagine trying to run a marathon but drinking no water the day before or during your race.

Christ compares Himself and the Holy Spirit to

water that quenches our spiritual thirst. Relationship with Christ--intimacy with His Spirit--satisfies the longing within our spirit. It is the water we need to survive spiritually. Without it, our spiritual vision blurs. Our spiritual muscles weaken and cramp. We become confused. Everything within our soul requires intimacy with God to be able to function well. It is from intimacy with God that all else flows. Psalm 1.2-3 tells us "but whose delight is in the Lord, and who meditates on His law day and night. That person is like a tree planted by streams of water, which yields its fruit in season and whose leaves do not wither--whatever they do prospers."

Your body cannot survive long without water, neither can your spirit survive without the water of eternal life.

For Further Study:

Water
Isaiah 44.3; John 3.5 & 7.37-39; Ephesians 5.25-27; 1 Corinthians 6.9-11; Titus 3.4-7

Day 28
Sacrifices

Do not offer any part of yourself to sin as an instrument of wickedness, but rather offer yourselves to God as those who have been brought from death to life; and offer every part of yourself to Him as an instrument of righteousness. Romans 6.13 (NIV)

No one likes to talk about it, but oftentimes our health requires sacrifice. Fitness is rarely achieved without it. The things we are holding onto are all too often the things holding us back. How many excuses have we made for not going on our long runs, skipping the gym in the morning, or forgoing that salad? The excuses are holding us back from the greatness that is held within. To unlock our fullest potential — to be the person God made us to be — we must sacrifice our excuses.

There is a lot that Abram/Abraham can teach us about sacrifice. When he was told to uproot his family and move to a new land, I imagine there were many good reasons not to do so. When he was told to place his son on an altar and literally sacrifice the boy to God, there were certainly good reasons to disobey

There is a cost. If we want to be healthy, the cost is our myriad of unhealthy habits. If we choose to eat junk and stay on the couch, it comes at the cost of our health. Put another way, if a bodybuilder wants to become leaner, they sacrifice pounds. If they want to gain more mass, they sacrifice unneeded calorie burn.

We must understand that our spiritual health, too, requires sacrifice. There are parts of culture that we may need to put down in order to see our spirits grow. There are relationships that must be laid upon the altar of spiritual health. There are even self-harming practices of over-committing and under-resting which need to be placed at the foot of the cross. Because one thing is for sure: intrinsic to growth and forward motion is a shedding of some things that are present.

For Further Study:

Sacrifice
> Luke 14.28; Romans 12.1; Hebrews 13.16; 1 Peter 1.6-7; Romans 5.8; John 3.16; Proverbs 21.3; Philippians 2.4

Day 29
Breathe

*But you will receive power when the Holy Spirit
comes on you; and you will be my witnesses in
Jerusalem, and in all Judea and Samaria, and to the
ends of the earth. Acts 1.8 (NIV)*

Oxygen is a fuel for our bodies. We need it in
our lungs, blood, brain, and muscles.

Runners know that the way in which they
breathe can make or break the quality of their
run. For instance, if you monitor your breathing-
-slowly inhaling through the nose and exhaling
through the mouth--you can sustain a faster pace
for longer intervals of time. Not to mention the
incredible positive impact it has on how we
physically feel during and after the run.

Slowly inhaling fills the lungs with oxygen and
gives them time to carry that oxygen into the
blood. It then gets transferred to the straining
muscles and sustains their ability to work.

πνεῦμα or pneuma* *(pnyoo'-mah)* is the Greek
word meaning breath.

Interestingly enough, it is also used to refer to
the Holy Spirit.

Like the body needs breath to function, so our

souls need breath. God's Spirit fills us and sustains us as we work for the Kingdom. Holy oxygen floods the soul and empowers spiritual exercises to continue.

Intentionally set time aside to spend intimately with God. Meditate on inhaling His Spirit and exhaling distractions. In every step, sync up with His will. Authentic, intimate relationship will fill the lungs of your soul and sustain the muscles in your spirit. Let us run the race that is marked out for us without forgetting to breathe.

For Further Study:

Breath of Life
Genesis 2.7; Job 33.4; 2 Samuel 22.16; Psalm 33.6 & 104.29; Acts 17.25

Holy Spirit
Isaiah 11.2 & 61.1; Joel 2.28; John 14.16 & 26, 15.26, & 16.7-15

Strong's Number 4145

Day 30
Pass it on

Therefore go and make disciples of all nations, baptizing them in the name of the Father and of the Son and of the Holy Spirit, and teaching them to obey everything I have commanded you. And surely I am with you always, to the very end of the age. Matthew 28.19-20 (NIV)

If going to the gym has transformed you into a healthier, happier person, you might invite friends to the gym with you. However, because of your transformation process, you know that it takes more than a gym membership to wholly remake a person. Dedication, sacrifice, and diligence all are necessary for meaningful transformation. Transformed people evangelize. They can't help but recruit.

Don't settle for new members. Become a disciple. Pass on your wisdom to the next generation. It is not enough to simply have new folks at church. We need more souls in heaven. You know the time and effort it takes. You know the challenges ahead. It would be irresponsible to encourage friends to join you at the gym and then leave them alone to aimlessly wander around, figuring things out on their own. Take time to shape the future by helping someone else's formation.

Paul, who wrote most of the New Testament, is a shining example of discipleship. In his letters to Timothy, we learn much about passing the baton. Jesus, too, spent years discipling young men. There are too many biblical examples of discipleship to count: Moses and Joshua; Naomi and Ruth; Eli and Samuel.

Continual spiritual development requires that we become light, shining on those around us (*Matthew 5.14-16*). Christ beckons us towards fruitfulness. We are to bear spiritual fruit, which houses spiritual seeds that fall onto soil and grow into new trees with new fruit to sow new soil. This is His plan for reconciliation.

For Further Study:

Pass it on

Psalm 145.4; Mark 1.16-22 & 3.13-15; Luke 4.18-19; John 13.15, 13.35, 15.8, & 21.15-19; Acts 1.8, 14.20-21, & 20.24; Romans 10.14-15; 1 Corinthians 11.1; 1 Peter 2.9-10; 2 Timothy 2.2; Hebrews 10.24-25

Christopher Qualls Publishing

www.ingramcontent.com/pod-product-compliance
Lightning Source LLC
LaVergne TN
LVHW041207080426
835508LV00008B/846